the book of

NOTHINGNESS

AMIT SINGH

Copyright © 2015 Amit Singh
All rights reserved

Healing Work LLC
Portland, OR

healingworkllc@gmail.com
booksofheart.com

isbn-13: 978-0692474259 (Healing Work LLC)
isbn-10: 0692474250

preface

The book of nothingness is not a book. It is my heart. It is my heart completely.

In that way, as I experience it, it is the heart of all people. It is our genuine heart, our real heart, our heart that belongs to all of us.

What do you belong to. Do you belong to yourself. Do you belong to freedom. Do you belong to certainty within yourself. Do you belong to knowledge within yourself.

This book is not a book. It is supposed to open up ability within you which can be done only by something that goes inside, penetrates you, and takes you where it is right for you to go.

This is what this book is for.

Love.

Amit Singh, 6/9/15, Portland, Oregon

the book of nothingness

Love is the only thing there

Do not think
Do not act
Do not be

Love is the only thing there

Love arises from openness within you
Love arises from emptiness within you
Love arises from the space within you
    where there is nothing at all

Love is the only thing there

Do not think at all in life
Thinking is not needed in the world
Thinking will bring suffering to you

Love is the only thing there

Do not act at all in life
Acting is not needed in the world
Acting will bring suffering to you

Love is the only thing there

Do not be at all in life
Being is not needed in the world
Being will bring suffering to you

Love is the only thing there

Be powerful here now
Be completely powerful here now

Power comes from your heart
Power comes from your spirit
Power comes from your soul
Power comes from the space in you

      where there is nothing at all

Love is the only thing there

Be happy here now
Be fully happy here now

Happiness comes from your heart
Happiness comes from your spirit
Happiness comes from your soul
Happiness comes from the space in you
      where there is nothing at all

Love is the only thing there

Be kind here now
Be fully kind here now

Kindness is a state of mind in you
It is the state in you
   in which life flows through you completely
You have no resistance to life then

Love is the only thing there

Be alive here now
Be fully alive here now

Aliveness is a state of mind in you
It is the state in you
   in which life flows through you completely
You have no resistance to life then

Love is the only thing there

Be open here now
Be open here fully and completely

Openness means that you are not
     there at all
Openness means that you are not there

        in a way
        that you don't even know
        you are not there

Love is the only thing there

Be open so fully
    that you are not there at all

Be open so completely
    that you have no awareness of your being

That is the state of being completely fearless in you
That is the state of being fully aware of who you are,
    and, at the same time
    having no over-awareness of your being

Love is the only thing there

Over-awareness is not needed
What is needed is simple awareness
Simple awareness of your surroundings
Simple awareness of your presence here
Simple awareness of life

Love is the only thing there

Simple awareness does not have a point of awareness
It just exists by itself
It just exists as if it is not there at all
It exists because it is not there

Because it is not there it is complete
Because it does not have a point of beginning
      and end,
        it is complete by itself

Love is the only thing there

To be simply aware you have to be nothing
To be nothing means

    to have no source in you
    to have no beginning or end in you
    to have no point of awareness
    to have no point of anything

Love is the only thing there

Life is a complete circle
It does not have a beginning
It does not have an end
It does not even have a shape

Love is the only thing there

To call life a circle
    means to call it something
    that is completely self contained
Calling life a circle
      does not mean that we are saying that
      life has a certain shape

It just means, that we are saying
    that life has no beginning, and no end
Of course, life can be circular,
    but, the circular nature of life
    includes every straight line possible

Love is the only thing there

Be open to life
Be fully open to life
Be kind to life
Be kind to others

You cannot tell who is going to be important to you
    when time has passed
If you look at people now,
    and they might look unattractive,
    or unkind,
    or having lack of joy in them,
    but, you cannot tell,

how quickly they might become
attractive, kind,
and capable of complete joy

Love is the only thing there

Do not think at all in life
Do not act at all in life
Do not be at all in life

Be powerful here now
Be completely powerful here now
Be completely powerful in a way
    that you are not powerful at all

Love is the only thing there

The power in you
    is the power of the being within you
The power in you
    is the power of the spirit within you
The power in you is the power of
    not knowing within you

Love is the only thing there

Not knowing is the greatest power inside you
It is the only power that is important
It is the only power that is needed in life
It is the only power that is relevant
It is the only power that is complete
It is the only power that is required in life

Love is the only thing there

Do not think at all in life
Do not act at all in life
Do not be at all in life

The power in you is the power of

    no power
The awareness in you is the awareness of
    no awareness
The joy in you is the joy of
    no joy
The quality in you is the quality of
    no quality

Love is the only thing there

When there is no quality in you,
    then, you have perfect quality in you
It is the lack of quality,
   that makes you a quality person
It is the lack of suffering in you
   that makes you a happy person

Love is the only thing there

Do not think at all in life
Do not act at all in life
Do not be at all in life

Be powerful here now

Be completely powerful here now
Be so powerful that you are not
    powerful at all

True power is nothing at all
It is just a state of mind
It is only a state of mind
It is the state of mind of
   total belief in you

Love is the only thing there

What is total belief
Total belief is the lack of belief
When you do not believe in anything,

       a space gets created in you
       which gives rise to primordial belief

Primordial belief is the state of being in you
       that is so complete,
       that there is no untruth in it

Love is the only thing there

Be happy here now
True happiness is the lack of happiness in you
It is the state of lack of any awareness of self
When self does not exist,
    there is no room for no happiness
Wherever there is self,
       there is going to be resistance of one kind
       or the other
When you have no self,
    no awareness of self,
    then you have total happiness
It is the absence of self that creates that space
Happiness is there,
       not because happiness is there,
       but, because there is no there-ness

Love is the only thing there

Be happy here now

Be fully happy here now
Be completely happy here now

Be open to life
Be completely open to life

True openness is nothing at all
It is nothing at all completely

True openness does not exist
For something to be open,
    there has to be something that is closed

There is nothing that is closed,
    so, there is nothing that is open
Reality is completely open,
        in a way that there is no openness,
        and there is nothing closed

Love is the only thing there

Reality is a full embrace,
        where there is nothing to embrace,
        but itself

There is nothing to embrace at all,
        because nothing is there

Because nothing is there,
        whatever is being sought for
        is not there at all

Love is the only thing there

What would it take for us,
        to stop seeking completely
It would mean to stop seeking
    happiness, joy, fulfillment,
    or whatever people seek

If there was no joy,
    or lack of joy,
    if, joy was a quality that was already present,
    we could give up all seeking completely

Love is the only thing there

In the end, there is nothing to seek at all
There is no seeker either

The seeker is an illusion
It is a complete illusion

In reality, the seeker does not exist

When we know that,
> when we have full awareness of that,
> when we have awareness of that,
> in a way that we have no awareness,
> the seeking stops completely

Love is the only thing there

What does it mean for seeking to stop completely
It means that there is no seeker,
   and nobody to seek
There is nothing at all

What does it mean to be nothing
What does it mean to be nothing
> in a way that
> there was never anything,
> and, there is no possibility of anything being there
> now or in the future

Love is the only thing there

Time does not exist at all
Time is perceived based in knowing
> that things happen based in time
There is a yesterday,
> there is today,
> and there will be tomorrow

When you are acutely aware of
> nothing being there at all,
> time loses its significance to the point that
> it absolutely disappears completely
It just retreats back into nothingness

Love is the only thing there

Time can be very difficult to understand,
> and get used to
In life, we live with time,

and we live with existence

To be fully creative in life,
    we have to have the perfect relationship with time
When we truly recognize that time has no existence,
    we become so creative,
        that, our creative force starts defining time,
        and starts creating time of its own

Love is the only thing there

Time can be created
Space can be created
You can create the life you want,
    as long as you know
    that there is no life,
    and there is no meaning in life

Love is the only thing there

When space and time do not limit you,
    when you do not have awareness of them,
    while you are living within them,
    you can change life to
    whatever you want it to be

Love is the only thing there

Be happy here now
Be completely happy here now

There is no time at all
There is no space at all
There was never ever time
There was never ever space

They are products of the mind
If you can understand your mind fully,
    you can control space,
    and, you can control time

Love is the only thing there

The art of controlling space and time,
    is to give up all control,
    and exist in
    no space,
    and no time

For people who have no space and no time,
    life gives them
    lots of space,
    and lots of time

Love is the only thing there

The art of controlling space and time,
    exists in uniqueness
It exists in recognizing your uniqueness,
    and bringing it forth in life

What is your uniqueness
Who are you as a person
What are you as a person
What are you capable of

What is the ability within you
    that is perfect and complete
What is the ability in you
    that is unique and beautiful
What is your nervous system capable of

Love is the only thing there

Everybody's nervous system is designed perfectly
It is designed for you to have certain tasks
    that are perfect for you
It fits in the world perfectly
It fits in the world so perfectly
    that you are perfect yourself

Love is the only thing there

Your nervous system can do anything you want to
You have to train it properly
There is a self training mechanism in your nervous system
You have to give it the right conditions though

Love is the only thing there

For the nervous system,
    the right conditions include
    sets of challenges,
    beliefs and requirements within you
    to have specific experiences in life

Life is designed to give you that
The only thing that is required is
    the ability to give up the familiar
    again and again

Love is the only thing there

What does it mean to give up the familiar
To give up the familiar
    is to give up security of every kind
    at any given stage of your life
Security means that you have stopped growing

Love is the only thing there

Your work is not to give you security
It is to give you satisfaction in life
Your work should give you satisfaction
It should give you satisfaction to your core

Love is the only thing there

What is your core
Your core is your set of values
Those are values that are integral to you
They are part of your nervous system

As you enliven your nervous system
   more and more
   through experiences that are perfect for you,
   those core values become more and more
   alive in you

Love is the only thing there

You have to live by those values
Those values are your intrinsic values
The way they are defined in you
    is perfect, and completely unique
It is not possible for two people,
   anywhere in the world
   to have the same core values
Because of the differences,
        we can contribute to life uniquely
        and become important members of society

Love is the only thing there

We should never give up
Sometimes, the hardest times
       are the most essential times
When we look back
       and see that we have powered though difficult times,
       we can see that the powering through has
       given us new meaning

Love is the only thing there

Be happy here now
Be fully happy here now

To have meaning in life,
   is to be able to contribute in life
To have full meaning in life,
   is to be able to contribute fully to life

In the end, there is no meaning to anything,
   yet, there is beauty to give to life

    in terms of meaning and relationships
That is what makes us perfect
We have to embrace both sides,
    the utter lack of meaning,
    and the ability to give full meaning
    in every way possible

Love is the only thing there

Do not think at all in life
Do not act at all in life
Do not be at all in life

Be powerful here now
Be completely powerful here now

Your search for meaning,
    comes from the place in your heart
    where there is no meaning at all

Love is the only thing there

Do not think at all in life
Do not act at all in life
Do not be at all in life

Your search for meaning is spontaneous to you
You do not have to think
    to have that search in you
You do not have to act
    to have that search in you
You do not have to be
    to have that search in you
It is spontaneous within you by itself

Love is the only thing there

Do not think at all in life
Do not act at all in life
Do not be at all in life

Your search for meaning is spontaneous in you
It is part of your personality
It is part of who you are
It is part of your nature
It is part of that in you
   which is nothing at all

Love is the only thing there

Be spontaneous here now
Be completely spontaneous here now

True spontaneity is in your heart always
It is the nature of your being
It is the nature of the person in you

To be authentic in yourself,
    you have to be spontaneous in your heart

Authenticity is the greatest tool you have
            in order to create meaning in your life

Love is the only thing there

What does it mean to be authentic
You have to search within yourself
     to know what the right tools are for you
     to use to express yourself in life
You have to find the tools that are authentic for you
If you are authentic as a person,
   you will find it really easy
That is why, authenticity
     is the greatest tool in you

Love is the only thing there

To be authentic,
   you have to know that,
   you cannot do anything
    to please other people
Do not try to please other people

If other people get pleased,
    because you are following your authentic self,
    then, it is fine
You should not try to please other people at all

Love is the only thing there

Authenticity requires courage
It requires you to give up trauma
It requires you to give up indolence
It requires you to give up hatred

It requires you to be normal
It requires you to be pleasant
It requires you to be simple

Love is the only thing there

Authenticity is not a war
There is nobody you are fighting against
If you are fighting against somebody,
    it is your own self you are fighting against,
    nobody else at all

Love is the only thing there

Stop fighting against yourself
Be open to life completely
Be open as if you are not open at all

Be complete as if you are not complete at all
Be kind as if you are not kind at all

Let things happen by themselves
Let things happen by themselves completely
Let things happen without happening at all

Love is the only thing there

The true way of letting things happen by themselves
    is to be so simple in your heart

    that you do not even know what is right,
    and what is wrong

Love is the only thing there

There is nothing that is wrong in life
There is nothing that is right in life

It is all a matter of perspective
What is the true perspective in life

There is no true perspective
In fact, the true perspective is no perspective

To give up all perspective,
    you have to become completely human
To be completely human,
    you have to embrace everything in life

You have to embrace sadness
You have to embrace ugliness
You have to embrace pain
You have to embrace beauty
You have to embrace your inability to change,
    when you need to change

Love is the only thing there

Be open to life
Be open to life fully

To be human,
    you have to embrace everything
You have to embrace your shortcomings
You have to embrace your talents

You have to embrace your inabilities
You have to embrace your abilities

Love is the only thing there

To be human completely,
    you have to give up all sadness,
    all pain, all suffering,
    because, as a human,
    you will attach yourself to
    what, in your own mind,
    has caused you all that suffering
    in your heart

Love is the only thing there

To be open completely,
    you have to know completely,
    that nothing has caused that
    suffering in your heart
    other than the nature of life itself

Love is the only thing there

When you can give up suffering completely,
    you are also saying that
      life is ok as it is

Life is ok as it is

Love is the only thing there

Life is ok as it is
You have to recognize that
If you can recognize that,
    then, you can go beyond life,
    then, you can go beyond suffering,
    then, you can go beyond space and time

Love is the only thing there

Life needs you
Life needs you
    to be you

Love is the only thing there

The art of giving to life,
    is the art of being in flow
Can you be in flow
Can you be in flow completely
Can you be in flow
    in a way that you are not there at all

Love is the only thing there

To be in flow,
    means, that you can spontaneously do
    what needs to be done in life
How beautiful is that life
    which is continuously in flow

Love is the only thing there

To be in flow can also mean
    to be in the zone

What does it mean to be in the zone
It means to act in a way
    that you don't even know that you are acting
Life comes to a standstill then
All your hopes and dreams come to a standstill then
You are so alive then,
    that you are not alive,
    you just are, as you are

Love is the only thing there

Do not think
Do not act
Do not be

Be powerful here now
Be completely powerful here now

To give to life,
    you have to be powerful
You have to be so powerful,

  that, you can withstand being in the zone
  for long periods of time

Love is the only thing there

To be in the zone means
  to give up all space and time
The energy that builds up in your body
  at that time is so powerful,
  that it can be compared to
  the primordial energy of life

Love is the only thing there

If you can withstand to be in the zone
 for long periods of time,
 you can create anything you want to in life

Love is the only thing there

To withstand being in the zone
  for long periods of time,
  you have to build up stamina
  and endurance

You have to be able to swim long,
  to run fast,
  to do tasks that are hard

 But, most importantly,
  you have to be able to do them
  without knowing that you are doing them

Love is the only thing there

Be open to life
Be completely open to life

Be open to life
 without being open to life

To be open to life fully
   you have to give up openness
You have to embrace unity in life

Unity means that everything is interconnected
There are invisible streams of consciousness
      that unite life so perfectly,
      that there is no unity either
There is total void in life

Love is the only thing there

The void is the space of invisibility
It arises from nothingness in you
It holds life in its lap
It is the area of awareness within you
It is the area of consciousness within you
It is the area of consciousness within you
   which does not have awareness of itself
You have to be doing all your work
    from that space
    in order to do the best work for you

Love is the only thing there

The void is the mother of life
It is what nurses life into existence

Love is the only thing there

The void is created by nothingness
Nothingness is not created by anything
It is its own creator,
   yet, it is its own creator,
   without there being any time
   when it was created,
   or, any time when it will be destroyed
It is free unto itself

Love is the only thing there

Be happy here now

Know nothing
Be nothing
Be aware of nothing

Do nothing
The highest form of doing work
    is to do nothing at all

When you do nothing,
    it is the void that is doing all the work

The void understands all life,
    so, when it does work,
    it does the work that is perfect for life

Love is the only thing there

Love is the space in the void
    where you need to exist all the time
Love is a space of falling within yourself
    and always feeling supported

Love is the only thing there

Love is the space of no judgement in you,
    yet, it maintains a sense of fairness in life

Love is the only thing there

Love is the space of not knowing in you,
    yet, it maintains a sense of normal knowledge in life

Love is the only thing there

Love is the space of adventure in you,
    yet, it retains a sense of familiarity in you

Love is the only thing there

Love is the space of power in you,
    yet, it remains vulnerable within itself

Love is the only thing there

Love is completeness in you,
    yet, it is always starting new things all the time

Love is the only thing there

Love is love in you,
    yet, at its heart,
    it is able to remain separate
    and unaffected by things

Love is the only thing there

Relationships are very important in us
Relationships survive because of listening
They prosper because of listening

The moment you reduce listening,
    your relationships reduce in quality
That is a law of life

Love is the only thing there

To listen better and better,
    you have to be open to life,
    and also able to wait in life

What does it mean to wait
To wait means to not give in to your emotions
    all the time

Love is the only thing there

Emotions are fractures within your consciousness,
    and they give color to life
The only problem is, when we prefer
    certain kinds of emotions over others

    again and again

It is ok to prefer certain emotions,
    but, to do it over and over again,
    causes stagnation of our personality,
    and hence, causes stagnation in our relationships,
    and hence, boredom in our relationships

Love is the only thing there

To destroy boredom,
    we have to re-invent ourselves

Any kind of re-invention requires us
    to look at things in a new way
In a way that is productive to us,
    and, in a way that is productive to life

Love is the only thing there

What is the way to make decisions

Decisions are based in listening
They are based in listening to the heart
They are based in listening to the self
They are based in listening to the void in us
But, in the end,
    they are based in listening to the nothingness in us

Love is the only thing there

The way to listen to nothingness
    is to give up listening,
    and embrace the nothing space in us
    which has no meaning,
    no form,
    nothing at all

Love is the only thing there

Only when we are comfortable with nothing,

    can we be people
    who can create value in life

To create value in life
   is the greatest quality within us
We have to do it,
   we have to reach for it,
   that is the only way
   for complete happiness to arise in us

Love is the only thing there

Complete happiness is not for ourselves
It has to be shared

When we share it
    we experience it fully

Love is the only thing there

Be happy
But, so not be happy
   because you have found happiness
But, be happy
   because you have found nothing

the process of creating this work

The process of creating this work was no process.

What does it mean by that.

When you get to a sweet spot in life where process does not matter, what you get is an empty space where anything is possible.

But, there is a process of how you get to that spot.

That is what this is about.

You cannot talk about love really. You can talk about its effects.

You can talk about the effects of love because you feel them. You feel them in your heart, you feel them in your spirit, you feel them in your soul.

But, you cannot talk about what exactly it is.

That is why it is impossible to talk about the space where the work happens or happened from.

But, what we will do, is try to have a conversation about what it is that we need to do in order to create work that is significant to our hearts.

I started thinking about writing a long time ago.

I started thinking about it in a way that a person thinks of mangoes, or grapefruit, or fine wine. The essence is the feeling of the fruit, the essence is what you feel within, it does not matter what the fruit is.

When you take a bite of a perfectly ripe mango, you know that you have entered a space that is complete, that it offers you all that you can take from it. There is nothing lacking in that space, nothing at all.

That is the beauty of life, of a grapefruit, or of fine wine. It offers you everything. It offers you the completeness of your being. There is nothing lacking in it at all.

I wanted to write like that. I wanted to write in completeness. I wanted to write as if, whatever was in front of you did not need to be there, yet, it was there in completeness.

A mango, does not need to be there. Within it, it does not show any hesitation at all. It is what it is. Similarly, when fine wine is drunk, you don't need to know where it came from, how it arose, why it arose. It might increase your experience, might bring you more joy in a certain way, but, in the moment of drinking it, all it needs to do is, stay still in your mouth, ready to be swerved in the way you wish to swerve it, ready to be swirled into your heart.

This book is like that. So, saying that I wrote it is immaterial and of no significance at all. It is totally true. I could take credit, or talk about the difficulties a person might encounter in the journey of life, I might sing my own praises in terms of how I subjugated my senses to come alive and produce this book fully. But, it would not be of significance completely.

Sometimes, a person wants to say some things anyway, and I will do that.

I have spent about 5-6 years working on this book. These 5-6 years have been spent, also, raising my kids, being a husband to my wife, running a healing practice, being a son, brother, what have you. I have done all those things while trying to write this book.

The fact that this book is here is a pure accident though. It might never have happened.

It happened because, one day, I stopped writing it.

I spent many mornings contemplating, finalizing, processing so many different versions of the book, that the one that came through in the end, was a total non-version.

I stilled my heart, and I said to myself, I am not going to write my book, I will just write with total meditation in my heart. And, a few hours later, the whole book was in front of me.

Not that I had not tried that way before, but, that morning, sitting at Pearl bakery, I completely gave up trying to write the book.

Sometimes, I can see, that in my healing practice, the best results happen when I am trying to do nothing and I succeed in doing that. Sometimes, our inner knowledge is so strong, that it guides us in unexpected ways to take us to the result that we expect from our hearts.

What is this game of expectation and non-expectation. It is hard to say what it is, but, it is a perfect thing in life.

Be perfect here my friends and just listen to what I am saying.

There is nothing wrong with you at all. To create a perfect thing, every process that you go through has to look imperfect and incomplete. In order to create something that is complete, you have to do a lot of incomplete things.

Do not forget that you are love in your heart, completely and fully.

When I started writing this book, I had just ordered myself a cookie and a coffee that I had put enough sugar in. I was happy. I was sitting by the window. My car was in the parking lot of Pearl bakery. Life was perfect.

Of course, if I had looked closer, I could have said that the window did not look over a majestic river, the seats were not so soft, and, maybe, my wallet did not have enough money.

But, does that matter. Maybe it does. I wouldn't know. I was able to produce a book in that space, occasionally looking up at people and smiling or saying hello to friends.

But, what does matter, I know very clearly is, that I did not question my state of mind. I did not question myself. I let it flow.

That is what is important.

What is flow though. Not questioning myself was flow at that time. Listening to my heart at that time was flow. I could have been afraid, and not believed in the work that was arising. I could have done that. I did not. That was flow.

It is possible, that 5-6 years of working on the book, and incessantly dreaming about it brought me to a state of flow in me, but, at that time, I did not need to be aware of that. I was that.

There is no need to be aware of what you are.

Too much self awareness would kill good wine, or kill the joy of drinking it. There is no need for that.

How to create a great thing then. Maybe, just let it happen.

What is the science of letting it happen. How does science see it.

How does science see reducing activity in the brain to the point that you are not functioning much, and then, using that to create that which is perfect.

The idea is, the brain has to be a conduit for love.

It has to be a conduit for perfection. For that to happen, we have to give up manufactured love, we have to give up manufactured perfection, ideas, faith, trust etc. We have to enter our heart, where the original of all those things sits. We have to wake up the original to create the truth in us.

Even if the truth is the same as other peoples' truth, the only way we can live it is by waking it in the heart.

Be in your heart today, now, forever.

What is truth anyway. Truth might be ease. Truth might be gratitude. Truth might be simplicity.

But, truth is never forceful. It is never rigid. It has the heart of compassion within itself.

Be truthful here.

When I was sitting and drinking my coffee, eating my cookie, and writing my book, I was very aware of who I was. But, the awareness of myself was not me as a separate person, but me as continuity of life.

So, yes, all works that are powerful, have to come from continuity of life. The more continuous life feels then, the more powerful the work will feel.

Continuity is very important in life. It is life itself. It is the basis of living. Any break in continuity breaks everything. Suddenly you have no life, and, life has to be started again. Those processes take a long time.

Love is the only thing there.

The continuity of life is the most important thing in life. It is the basis of living. It is the basis of joy in life.

Continuity in narrative is very important in books. If there is no continuity, the book is very hard to read, or it can be completely unreadable. Sometimes, there is a ruse to writing, where a person uses breaking of continuity in order to tell a story. That is fine if it is done well, and that the continuity is carried on in some other way.

There might be continuity of style then, or continuity of emotion, or continuity of idea. If that is not the case, then, the book would be a very badly written book, and you could try reading something else instead.

The idea of writing is that you have to write like a melody, like a quality in the book that says that I have been loved.

If that is not the case, then what is the use.

The book should have been loved by the writer. That is the basis of living. That is the basis of the work.

There are books that are not loved by writers. That is ok, as long as those books are considered essential in one way or the other. Something that which is considered essential is being loved, though not in the way we love something through our hearts, but, instead, through our minds.

Essential things are important to life. Even if they are not loved fully, they still fulfill a deep purpose in our lives.

Books that are not considered essential by the writers and not loved also, should not be there at all. They are just trash, nothing else.

Life is beautiful and perfect. We have to see it like that.

We have to see life as perfect. We have to love life, or consider it essential.

Whatever work we do, we have to think that it is essential to us, to life, to humanity, or to people around us, or we have to love it with our hearts.

The idea of love comes from the heart.

When you want to produce something, anything, that you care about, you have to go into your heart and truly understand what it is. When you do that, you will be completely satisfied with your process, and, you will be very happy with the work you do.

In the end, work is nothing. It does not matter that this book exists, or anything in the world exists. The world is a mirage, a complete mirage, and, if we understand it like that, we will only do work that is essential or work that we love.

It is because we think the world is real that we do work that is inconsequential and trashy. If you want to do good work, you have to believe the world to be not real.

But, what does that non-reality mean. It means that it comes from a space that does not exist, so, the world, in its true essence, has no existence at all.

There is no failure, and no success at all. If a person is like that, and feels like that, then every moment they live, they will put total value in it.

The chasing after total value is not a chasing at all. It is a real thing based in the fact that the world does not exist at all.

The reality of the world is love, which is not something that exists at all. In reality, the word love does not exist, and the idea of love does not exist. Even the emotion of love does not exist.

Love is a thing that does not exist. It is the presence of not-ness in us.

Not-ness is nature. It is love truly.

So, when I sat at Pearl bakery, and I sat at that window, and I sat with my coffee and cookie, and sat with nothing in my heart, and I opened the heart's door, and let the words arise from nothingness in me, I was within not-ness and within that which is nothing.

I was able to create then, as if, I was not creating.

Love is the only thing there.

Amit Singh, 6/16/2015, Portland, Oregon

meditation

the art of living is the art of non-being
non-being is the root of all life
all life is based in non-being

to not be is the greatest truth in life
how to not be
let it happen spontaneously
do not rush it
do not make effort

love is the only thing there

amit singh
7/1/15
portland, or

www.ingramcontent.com/pod-product-compliance
Lightning Source LLC
Chambersburg PA
CBHW061347040426
42444CB00011B/3129